James Granville Add

The Fight for the Drama

James Granville Adderley

The Fight for the Drama at Oxford

ISBN/EAN: 9783743320338

Manufactured in Europe, USA, Canada, Australia, Japa

Cover: Foto ©ninafisch / pixelio.de

Manufactured and distributed by brebook publishing software
(www.brebook.com)

James Granville Adderley

The Fight for the Drama at Oxford

THE

FIGHT FOR THE DRAMA

AT

OXFORD

SOME PLAIN FACTS NARRATED BY

The Hon. and Rev. J. G. ADDERLEY

WITH A PREFACE BY

W. L. COURTNEY, M.A.

OXFORD:

B. H. BLACKWELL, 50 & 51, BROAD STREET.

LONDON:

SIMPKIN, MARSHALL, AND CO.

—

1888.

OXFORD:
PRINTED BY E. B. DOE,
126A, HIGH STREET.

TO THE

O. U. D. S.

AUTHOR'S NOTE.

Nothing but the request of my Oxford acting friends would have made me consent to the publication of this paper, and I think it is right to inform my readers of it that in its original form it was an address delivered before the members of the Church and Stage Guild and was not intended for printing. If, however, its publication in any way serve to help the removal of any prejudice which may still exist against University acting, I shall be amply repaid and shall not mind being charged with the many literary blemishes which I am painfully aware disfigure the pages which follow.

J. G. A.

AVANT-PROPOS.

WHETHER the modern dramatic movement is or is not beneficial, is much debated in the common rooms of Oxford. The establishment of a new theatre is looked on with suspicion by those who believe that one more expedient has been invented for distracting and dissipating the undergraduate's time. But of all opposition to the theatre, the most unreasonable is that of those senior members of the University who, without any compunction of conscience, quietly permitted the vulgarities and indecencies of the Victoria Theatre. Every term the "Vic" used to be the chosen home of Vance,

Jolly Nash, *et hoc genus omne;* nothing
more refining than a music-hall entertainment was ever allowed to be exhibited
on boards which would presumably have
been defiled by a stage play. Only during
the vacation, when the University veto
was removed, was the Victoria Theatre
ever respectable. The New Theatre is
an enormous improvement on all this,
and it in reality rests with the ladies
and gentlemen of Oxford to make it
what they please. Mr. Irving made
some remarks on this subject in his
recent Discourse, which are worth
quoting :—

In the course of my training, long
before I had taken what I may call my
degree in London, I came to act in
your city of Oxford. I have a very

pleasant recollection of the time I passed here, though I am sorry to say that, owing to the regulation which forbade theatrical performances during term-time, I saw Oxford only in vacation, which is rather like—to use the old illustration—seeing "Hamlet" with the part of *Hamlet* left out. There was then no other building available for dramatic representations than the Town Hall. I may, perhaps, be allowed to congratulate you on the excellent theatre which you now possess— I do not mean the Sheldonian—and at the same time to express a hope that, as a more liberal—and might I say a wiser ?—régime allows the members of the University to go to the play, they will not receive any greater moral injury or be distracted any more from their studies than when they were only allowed the occasional relaxation of hearing comic songs. Macready once said that "a theatre was a place of recreation for the sober-minded and intelligent." I trust that under whatsoever management the theatre in Oxford may be it will always deserve this character.

But if doubts are felt on the subject of a respectable theatre, still greater apprehensions are entertained as to the existence of an Undergraduate Dramatic Club. Possibly there was much the same division of feeling when the Undergraduates of the seventeenth century acted before King James, and Drs. Gwynne and Barten Holyday and Jasper

Fisher were very likely suspected, like
Socrates, of "corrupting the minds of the
young." *Adhuc sub judice*—the experiment
is still on its trial. But there are two
points at least to be considered by the
opponents of the amateurs. In the first
place, do what we will, we cannot alter
human nature : and nature in a body of
some 2000 Undergraduates is sure to
produce a considerable proportion of men
who have the histrionic instinct. In the
second place, if the first point be granted,
it seems to follow that public recognition
is infinitely better than official prohibition.
For what is the alternative to a respectable and recognised dramatic society ?
A secret club, leading an underground
existence, without the possibility of any

serious criticism and therefore for ever
tending to the lower forms of drama.

W. L. COURTNEY.

THE FIGHT FOR THE DRAMA AT OXFORD.

THE fact that in 1836 the Undergraduates of Oxford were liable by statute to be flogged if they looked at a Punch and Judy show in the street, while in 1886 Mr. Irving gave a lecture on that most wicked art of Acting, in the very presence and at the special request of the Vice-Chancellor himself, in the sacred precincts of the New Schools, is a sign of fifty years' progress which alone might justify a Jubilee celebration.

I propose to give a short narration of facts which may serve to make clear how this great change has come about.

We all feel that of late years Society has been realizing more and more that acting is a part of our very nature, and that you might just as well try to abolish eating and

B

drinking as try to put an end to the Stage and the Drama. Nay more, Society has begun to recognise that the art of acting is not merely a necessary evil or a harmless amusement, but a real good: an art that creates as well as recreates. But, for some reason or other, Oxford University has taken longer than any other portion of society to accept the new gospel of the Drama.

Cambridge has been very much better in this respect. She has allowed her Undergraduates to act during the last thirty or forty years, but in Oxford the battle is only just won.

I lack the wit of Mr. Burnand, and cannot hope to narrate in these notes, hurriedly jotted down in the midst of other work, with comparatively little matter at my disposal, anything so interesting or so amusing as his " Reminiscences of the A.D.C." But I will tell you just the facts, as I have learnt them, of the history of the Drama at Oxford, and as I knew them when I was there myself.

When I was at Oxford between the years 1870 and 1882, we used to be told that such a thing as an acting Undergraduate was altogether an anomaly; he was forbidden by the statutes; he had never existed and must never do so. But these statements were quite contrary to fact. Any one who has read old histories of Oxford and Cambridge, is well aware that in the good old days, before Puritanism got the ascendancy, University theatricals were as common as water.

We still have the text of plays in Latin and English, which were written and acted by members of the University, in the presence of Kings and Queens of the 16th and 17th centuries. When Queen Elizabeth visited Oxford in 1566, and again in 1592, it was customary to produce plays on Sunday evenings in Christ Church Hall. On the first of the two visits, a Latin play called " Progne," by a Canon of Christ Church, was produced. On the same occasion, an English play, called " Palæmon and Arcyte," written by R. Edwards, was acted, in which a real pack of hounds was introduced into Tom quad to lend effect to a hunting scene. The audience were so excited when the hounds gave tongue that they ran out into the quad, and left the play to go on by itself. Real scenery is said to have been first introduced at these Christ Church performances. It was also during the acting of " Palæmon " that a fall of the stage disabled some of the actors, and the Queen sent the Vice-Chancellor behind the scenes to help those who were hurt! A short sketch of these ancient performances was given by Mr. Courtney in the November, 1886, number of *Time*, and full particulars are to be found in old books.

In the reign of James I. we read that a play entitled " Vertumnus " was performed by the Scholars of St. John's, three of whom came out to meet him habited as witches, and foretold a long and happy reign to the king.. Charles I., too, was fond of witnessing performances in Christ Church Hall.

At Cambridge so much was acting en-
couraged, that in 1535 nine lecturers of
Trinity were ordered by statute to act
publicly every Christmas on pain of 10s.
fine for non-compliance.

But from the beginning of the last century
to the middle of this, my catena of dramatic
performances presents a formidable gap.
With the exception of some scattered refer-
ences in the *Gentleman's Magazine*, I do not
think there is any record of efforts in the
right direction till the year 1845.

About the year 1845, Oxford was passing
through one of her witty periods, which are
now, alas! so unfrequent. Now-a-days, the
art of satire and epigram seems almost lost
at the Universities. Since the days of
Calverley's Poems, I do not think anything
in that line has been written which is likely
to survive the test of time. But forty years
ago it was a different story. Those were
the days of the " Art of Pluck " and the
" Hints to Freshmen," followed in 1869 by
the " Oxford Spectator " and the " Tatler."

And side by side came, as it generally does, the desire for the Drama, the desire that is, to put wit into action. B.N.C. must have the credit of being the first college to start theatricals. The late Frank Talfourd, together with 'some B.N.C. Undergraduates, many of whom have since become famous both in pulpit and stage, started a society called the "Oxford Dramatic Amateurs." They did not act very much in Oxford, but generally gave their performance at Henley during the Regatta week, in much the same way as the Old Stagers—the leading amateur club, incorporated with the celebrated I Zingari—give their performances at Canterbury during the annual cricket week in August.

Their first public venture was in 1847, when a burlesque by Frank Talfourd entitled "Macbeth Travestie" was performed, with the author as *Lady Macbeth*, and Samuel Brandram as *Macbeth*. The entertainment concluded with "Bombastes Furioso," in which Mr. Brandram actually danced. A picture of the *pas de quatre* danced on this occasion, made by George Augustus Sala, was for some time in the possession of a friend of mine, a country clergyman, to whom I am indebted for these facts.

In the same year, these Dramatic Amateurs performed at the London residence of Mr. Talfourd in Russell Square, in the presence of Charles Dickens, John Leech, Albert Smith, the Keeleys, and other distinguished persons. The following year, 1848, " Ion," by Mr. Talfourd's father, was performed at B.N.C. This was probably the first public dramatic entertainment given by Undergraduates in Oxford during this century. I have not been able to discover in what light the authorities regarded it. It is interesting to note that the A.D.C. at Cambridge was founded just about this time. My informant also tells me that this performance of " Ion" at B.N.C. was very near being a failure because Cust, an Undergraduate of the

College, now better known as Dean of York, in true amateur style, threw up his part (a very important one) at the last moment, in order to go to the Queen's ball.

In 1849 the Amateurs went a step further and came to London, took Miss Kelley's (the old Royalty) Theatre, and acted " Macbeth Travestie" and "Box and Cox," preceded by a drama in which Sam Brandram and Mrs. Fanny Stirling acted.

In 1850 another Oxford performance was got up. " Thumping Legacy " was put into rehearsal, but for some reason or other was given up. In this rehearsal the part of *Jerry* was assigned to Mr. Edmund Yates, and that of *Rosetta* to Mr. Charles Kegan Paul. As a substitute for " Thumping Legacy," " Box and Cox " was acted. As an *entr'acte*, Mr. Sam Brandram sang " Caller Herrin'," and the performance concluded with a burlesque, of " Hamlet," written by Hole, of B.N.C., now Dean of Rochester, in which the part of *Polonius* was taken by Cust, who this time had no State ball to attract him elsewhere. Here we have an early instance of the connection of the Church and Stage; indeed, I have always noted that there is a remarkable similarity between the names of those who were celebrated for amateur acting at the University and those who are now prominent ministers of the Church. Here we have two Very Rev. Deans of the Church, one writing a burlesque and the other playing in it, and, I have no doubt, dancing. A right rev. Prelate, lately deceased, was a brilliant actor when at Cambridge; another well-known Canon was Mr. Burnand's right hand in establishing the A.D.C. The *première danseuse* at Oxford in my day is now a Priest; no less than nine of those with whom I acted when an Undergraduate are now ordained.

To return to Oxford. Fired by the success of the B.N.C. Amateurs, we now find Balliol taking up the work. The leading spirits in this new enterprise were Mr. Herman Merivale and Mr. Robert Reece.

In 1850, to the horror of the authorities at Balliol, a performance was given of two farces, "To Oblige Benson" and "Crinoline," the cast of which contained, besides the names of Herman Merivale and Robert Reece, those of Edmund Warre, now the Head Master of Eton; W. Jackson, now Rector of Exeter College, Oxford; D. Fearon, H.M. Inspector of Schools; S. Hills, now a Judge in Ireland; and T. H. Escott, the late Editor of the *Fortnightly Review.* A full account of this performance was contained in an article in the *Theatre* last year, by Mr. Reece. No great advance seems to have resulted from this performance, and I do not know that anything more was done for 16 years, but in 1866 the "Shooting Stars," a more important society than any hitherto started in Oxford, was formed; some of the best actors of the day were members of this society. I have no complete record of all the Shooting Stars' performances, but here are some: on July 8th, 1866, they acted the " Comical

Countess" and "Lalla Rookh" (burlesque) in the Masonic Hall. In November, 1866, they played "Dearest Mamma" and "Fair Helen" at the Victoria Music Hall (as it was then most properly termed). In February, 1868, they performed "Wonderful Woman" and "Lurline" at the "Vic." Mr. Vincent Amcotts generally wrote the burlesque.

During the same period an excellent society was formed at St. John's College, under the management of Mr. E. Nolan, who was associated with Bishop Copleston and Mr. T. Humphry Ward in the "Oxford Spectator." The St. John's Society went in for comedies and burlesques. During the years 1866, 1867, and 1868, they played "The Rivals," "She Stoops to Conquer," "Scrap of Paper," "Still Waters run Deep," also "Iphigenia" and "Romeo and Juliet" burlesques.

Unfortunately, the "Shooting Stars," chiefly owing to the persistent opposition of the authorities, who drove the members into a system of doing everything *sub rosâ*,

fell into great disrepute; in fact some of the
members were undoubtedly connected with
a great London scandal in the year 1869-70.
This was almost the death blow to acting in
Oxford. With the exception of a splendid
attempt by Mr. Stephen Gatty (son of the
authoress) and Hon. Alex. Yorke, which
was defeated by the Dean of Christ Church,
then Vice-Chancellor, nothing further, as
far as I know, was tried till we began our
battle in 1879.

When I came up to Oxford in 1879, the
only entertainment provided for our amusement was a Music Hall performance at the
" Vic "—and I say unhesitatingly that the
" Vic " was the most disgusting place of
entertainment I ever had the misfortune to
attend. The audience consisted of so-called
Oxford gentlemen in their very worst form.
The occupants of the stalls never scrupled
to pelt the performers with any nasty thing
they chanced to have in their hands or their
heads; no respect of any kind was shown to
the ladies and gentlemen of the profession

who performed. And this was allowed by the very same authorities who persistently refused to allow the Legitimate Drama to be performed, either by professionals or amateurs during term time. It was considered safer for the morals of the Oxford Undergraduate that he should spend his evenings at the " Vic," than that he should run the risk of contamination by witnessing, or taking part in, a play of Shakspeare, Sheridan or Goldsmith.

Most right-minded people in Oxford were getting heartily sick of this state of things ; squibs and caricatures appeared in Shrimpton's windows, showing the absurdity of the position, letters were written to the papers, and the matter was discussed in common-rooms.

In December, 1879, some of us Undergraduates at Christ Church thought we would try and start a society similar to the A.D.C. at Cambridge. I do not think at the time we half realized the prejudice then existing in Oxford against any such attempt.

We began in a small way; we issued invitations to our friends in Christ Church to witness a performance in my rooms in Peckwater. The programme consisted of the "Area Belle," imitations of popular actors, and the inevitable "Box and Cox." The greatest consternation prevailed among the authorities at the sight of scenery and footlights being publicly carried through the College gates. The Censors were dismayed, but hardly knew how to stop it. Unable to prevent our acting, they resolved to starve us. There is an ancient rule in Christ Church that not more than four supper rations are allowed to each person. I wanted supper for 40, and accordingly made a special application, which was indignantly refused. But in Christ Church, where regulations abound, means of evading them are also plentiful; and the supper rule can be beautifully evaded in this way—though only four suppers are allowed, you can have as many to lunch as you like. Who then could prevent our ordering 40 luncheons and keeping them in a cool place till midnight, after the play, when we could eat them and call them suppers? In this way the Censors were non-plussed, and both theatricals and supper came off with the greatest possible éclat. It is pleasing to contrast this opposition of the Censors then, with the fact that recently a similar performance was given in a Christ Church Undergraduate's room, at which several Dons were present, and to which the full approbation of the same Censor was given. A few days after this performance we were invited to the Deanery to give an entertainment to the late Duke of Albany; our scenery was carried in triumph to the Deanery: the Vice-Chancellor, was among the audience. A full account appeared in the local papers, and we awoke to find ourselves famous.   .

We organized ourselves into a Society called the Oxford Philothespians, and set about to prepare for a public performance the following term. We decided to go straight to the Vice-Chancellor and ask for

permission. I was not present at this, the
first interview of the Society with the Vice-
Chancellor, so I cannot describe it, but from
all accounts it was not so romantic as that
described by Mr. Burnand in his Reminiscences with the Vice-Chancellor of Cambridge, who thought Βοξ καὶ Κοξ Fellows of
Trinity.

Dr. Evans, of Pembroke, who was the
Vice-Chancellor of our day, refused his permission.   He said, " You may do what
you like in your Colleges as far as I am
concerned, but publicly I forbid you to
act."   We took this as including *lodgings*
which, in a certain sense, are part of the
Colleges, and we determined to perform at
No. 26, Cornmarket, the residence of one of
our members, Mr. Gilbart Smith.   Here, in
June, 1880, we performed " Içi on parle
Francais," the Screen scene from " School
for Scandal," and " Villikins and his Dinah,"
to crowded audiences, for two nights;
among the performers being Mr. Elliott
Lees (now M.P. for Oldham), Mr. Avray

Tipping, Mr. Alan Mackinnon, and Mr. (now the Rev.) Hubert Astley. We charged five shillings for admission, and the demand for tickets was enormous. We were informed afterwards that the Proctors came to the door of the house, but on hearing that certain distinguished academic ladies were present, thought it better not to interfere, and accordingly retired.

Next term, Michaelmas, 1880, we again resolved to approach the Vice-Chancellor. This time I addressed a letter to the great man, and asked him to give his serious attention to the subject of dramatic performances in Oxford, pointing out to him that while he tolerated the "Vic," it was absurd to discountenance us. No answer being vouchsafed to this epistle I called on him with our Secretary. He emphatically refused his patronage or sanction to the Society. Nothing daunted, we prepared for another performance, and in February, 1881, played "Dearer than Life" (Mr. Toole's great piece), and a

c

burlesque called "Lord Lovell" at the Templar's Hall.

However, having once given a thoroughly public performance without rebuke, we were emboldened to come out in full force at the next Commemoration. We accordingly, in the Summer Term, 1881, took the Holywell Music Room, the largest place available, and announced two performances of the " Clandestine Marriage." But this time the Vice-Chancellor was aroused. He sent for us a few days before the entertainment and remonstrated. We said we were very sorry, but having performed in public the term previous, we thought we might do it again. Then he showed his kind-heartedness. He knew we had put ourselves to a great deal of trouble, and gave us permission to act— this was the only time we ever got it— but his permission was coupled with a solemn charge that we must never do it again. We thanked him, and rushed from his presence to order a thousand circulars, .headed with the magic words " By permission of the Vice-Chancellor." The effect was wonderful. About 400 tickets were sold; Heads of Colleges, even Proctors, came, and all seemed happy. Only when it was all over, came the deadening feeling that it was the last time of performance—we were forbidden to act again.

Meanwhile a sudden and startling impulse was given to the Drama by the production of a Greek Play in Balliol Hall, under the immediate patronage of the Master, Mr. Jowett. The idea was so novel and so piquant alike to the classical scholar and the histrionic undergraduate, that " Agamemnon " fairly took Oxford by storm, and when represented at St. George's Hall, Langham Place, caused considerable interest even in the metropolis. The principal parts were taken by Messrs. Benson, Lawrence, Bruce, and Courtney, the chorus-music being composed by Mr. Parratt. This performance, though it can hardly be said to be the forerunner of the present movement, yet undoubtedly had a great effect. It showed the authori-

ties that Undergraduates could be perfectly
serious and artistic in getting up theatricals.

During the remainder of the year, 1881,
we contented ourselves with small private
performances in our club room. In the early
part of 1882, we made a new departure, and
acted at the Bicester Town Hall. These
served to keep our name before the public,
and secretly we were determined not to be
crushed. We felt we had a good cause to
fight for, namely, to break down prejudice
against the Drama. We knew that half the
University was with us, and that it was only
a question of time; and if we do appear to
many to have defied the Vice-Chancellor
and his edicts—I confess it looks like it—
I can only plead the nature of our cause as
our justification.

When the Midsummer Term arrived, we
felt that a blow must be struck. A performance must be given at Commemoration or
the thing might die out and all our work be
thrown away. By a providential coincidence
at this time a new Senior Proctor came into

office, the Rev. H. Scott Holland, now
Canon of St. Paul's. I had heard vague
rumours that, when he was young, he was a
celebrated amateur actor, and I determined
to get him on my side and work a performance through his influence. I laid the
case before him; I told him what the Vice-
Chancellor had said the year before, but
suggested that if we gave our performance
in a rather more private manner, perhaps he
would not object. Mr. Holland threw himself heart and soul into the matter, inter-
viewed the Vice-Chancellor and told him
all about it. Again Dr. Evans' kind-
heartedness struggled with his conviction of
the wickedness of acting. He said "he
would rather not be applied to; if the performance was really going to be private he
would say nothing, but if the matter was
directly brought under his notice he must
say—'no.'" Armed with this half permission
we proceeded to put two plays into rehearsal—"Husband to Order" and "Little Tod-
dlekins."

When, however, we sent round our circulars announcing the performance, some kind Don sent one to the Vice-Chancellor, calling his attention to the fact that men were going to dress up in ladies' clothes, and that we were charging five shillings for admission. Now this was just what Dr. Evans did not want, but it was done, and he could not avoid it. Mr. Holland was sent for—" They are acting against my authority," said Dr. Evans. " Yes, but it is quite private," said the Senior Proctor. " I don't care," said the Vice-Chancellor, " I shall have to send somebody down—it has been brought under my notice, and I must do something." However he did nothing. So we proceeded with rehearsals, when, lo! on the morning of the performance I received a terrible letter, which read as follows :—

" The Vice-Chancellor considers that the performance announced in the Holywell Rooms is a breach of the Statutes, and a contempt of his authority, and, therefore, requests Mr. Adderley to call upon him on Thursday at 12 o'clock."

Here was I going to act at two o'clock that day, Saturday, but with the command of the Vice-Chancellor to appear before him on the following Thursday, to be sent down in disgrace from the University! It was 10 o'clock, there was no time to lose. I resolved to go and confront him. Previously Mr. Holland had most kindly called on Dr. Evans to plead for me, and assure him that I was not quite so wicked as a " Shooting Star." I went to Pembroke. " The Vice-Chancellor is out, but will be in at one o'clock," said the servant. One o'clock!—only an hour before the curtain was timed to rise. One o'clock came, and I was ushered into his presence. " Haven't you got my letter?" he said; "why do you come here? you must come next Thursday." " No, Dr. Evans," I said, " I cannot wait till next Thursday. I hear you are going to send me down: I want to know if this is true before

I go and act. I shall not act if you are going to send me down." "How do you know I am going to do anything of the kind?" said he. "I have been told so," I said. "Is it true? because I don't intend to act if it is." I decline to answer, sir; you must come on Thursday; I cannot speak to you."

With a heavy heart, I left the room, and proceeded to the Holywell Music Room, to play *Madame Phillipeau* in the "Husband to Order," and *Amanthis* in "Little Toddle-kins." I spent a very miserable five days, as you may imagine, but the end was satisfactory. Thanks almost entirely to the Senior Proctor, Dr. Evans was persuaded to look kindly on the matter. It was his last day of office when he sent for me. "I am glad," he said, "not to have to do anything disagreeable, as this is my last day of office; I shall not trouble you any more after to-day. Good-bye,"—and he shook hands.

The accession to office of Mr. Jowett, the Master of Balliol, in the Michaelmas Term,

1882, marks a new era in the Drama at Oxford. From this time we were as free as when we first began, but with ˙a vast additional strength in the way of celebrity and popularity. It was also at this time that the cleverest actor we ever had, and one, were he to adopt the Stage as a profession, likely to make his name famous hereafter, Mr. Arthur Bourchier, came up from Eton to Christ Church. An amateur of rare flexibility and talent, with all the enthusiasm of a Freshman, he threw himself into the work just when most of us were occupied in reading for our Final Schools, and it is mainly due to his energy and determination at a most critical time, that the numerous obstacles and prejudices which existed in many undergraduate quarters at that time towards establishing the Drama have since been removed.

The first question of importance which arose was what attitude should we adopt towards the Vice-Chancellor. The attitude we decided to adopt was bold, not to say

patronizing. We sent Mr. Jowett an invitation to come to a grand performance of
" Money" in the Holywell Music Room. At
any rate this had the result of bringing the
whole matter to a head at once. Mr. Jowett
sent for me. Once more I threw myself on
Mr. Holland—I implored him to persuade
the Vice-Chancellor to give us his sanction—
I was ordered to be at Balliol at 12 the next
day; I asked Mr. Holland to go there at
11.30, and have half-an-hour's talk with the
Vice-Chancellor before I came. That half-
hour's talk decided the fate of the Drama at
Oxford. I attribute it almost entirely to the
persuasiveness of Mr. Holland at his interview with Mr. Jowett, that when I arrived
at 12 o'clock the Vice-Chancellor received
me with the greatest courtesy, and ap-
pointed a meeting of the Committee of
the Philothespians at his house on the
following day, at which his now famous
decision was given, which forms the basis
of the modern recognition of acting at
Oxford.

The decision was this:—Mr. Jowett first of all sanctioned our performance of " Money " at the Holywell Rooms, which, preceded by a prologue and a farce, was given four times in two days—by invitation—Mr. Bourchier as *Sir John Vesey*, Mr. W. H. Spottiswoode as *Glossmore*, Mr. Goring Thomas as *Stout*, Mr. Lushington as *Lady Franklin*, Mr. (now the Rev.) C. J. Shaw as *Clara Douglas*, and Mr. F. Glyn as *Georgina*, being very successful. He then agreed to allow us to act publicly in Oxford for the future on two conditions. (1) We must act Shakspeare only. (2) Ladies must take the female characters.

In the Summer Term of 1882, the Philothespians contented themselves with Smoking Concerts and small private performances— I can only now speak as an outsider, for my Oxford days were over, and my Degree taken.

In December, 1883, a performance of the " Merchant of Venice " took place in the Town Hall, preceded by a prologue written by Mr. F. E. Weatherly, and recited by me. This was the first performance of one of Shakspeare's plays ever undertaken by members of the Universities and presented in a University Town before an Academic audience. It excited the greatest interest within Oxford itself, and was extensively commented on in the public newspapers, which all gave great assistance in encouraging the movement; the most noteworthy article being written by the well known dramatic critic of the *Daily Telegraph*, Mr. Clement Scott; and amongst the audience were to be found many whose sympathies had never before been extended towards dramatic efforts in Oxford, including the Vice-Chancellor, the Dean of Christ Church, President of Trinity, President of Magdalen, Master of University, and the Warden of All Souls (Sir William Anson, a distinguished amateur actor in his undergraduate days). Mr. Bourchier produced the play and acted *Shylock*, a performance which brought him rich and well-deserved laurels. *Launcelot*

Gobbo was capitally played by Mr. Bromley Davenport (now M.P. for Macclesfield), while *Gratiano* by Mr. A. M. Mackinnon, the *Duke of Venice* by Mr. W. J. Morris, *Antonio* by Mr. (now the Rev.) E. G. Gordon, and *Bassanio* by Mr. W. L. Courtney, were no less successful impersonations. But perhaps the most striking element in the production was the active co-operation of ladies in the parts of *Portia*, *Nerissa*, and *Jessica*,—Mrs. Woods (wife of the President of Trinity) was *Jessica*, Miss Arnold *Nerissa*, and Mrs. W. L. Courtney and Miss E. Arnold played *Portia* on alternate evenings. It must be distinctly pronounced a great success ; the Town Hall was crowded for six nights and one morning performance, and the play was repeated twice at the Memorial Theatre, Stratford-on-Avon, at Leamington, and at Charterhouse School, in the vacation. The Vice-Chancellor came in state ; in fact, during the whole of his Cancellariate, Mr. Jowett was a regular attendant at Undergraduate theatricals.

But the first Shaksperian performance was also the last *Philothespian* performance; it was felt that the movement had grown so big that nothing but a *University* Society would satisfy its requirements. Therefore, at a meeting in Mr. Bourchier's rooms in Christ Church, the Club was re-founded and called the Oxford University Dramatic Society, which it remains to this day.

In 1884, no performance was given, but in May, 1885, " Henry IV.," Part I., was played at the Town Hall. A prologue, written by Mr. G. N. Curzon, M.P., (whose attitude towards the House of Lords is now gaining so much attention in the public press), was spoken by Mr. Lang (President of the Union). Although the plot is not as interesting as many of Shaks-speare's, it is admirably suited to a Club, and was a happy choice for the inaugural performance of the O.U.D.S. Mr. Mac-kinnon produced the play and played *Prince Hal*, Mr. Gilbert Coleridge was *Falstaff*, Mr. Bourchier *Hotspur*, Mr. E. Harington the

King, Mr. Mitchell-Innes *Poins*, Mr. H. V. Page (Captain of the 'Varsity Eleven) *Bardolph*, and Mr. S. E. R. Lane *Douglas ;* the last-named gentleman was an excellent Secretary, and together with Mr. Grant Asher, a celebrated 'Varsity Blue, was very instrumental in helping the reconstitution of the Club. Mrs. Woods, Lady St. Leonards, and Lady Edward Spencer Churchill (who sang the Welsh song, "Bells of Aberdovey," most charmingly), gave great assistance, and the battle scenes were admirably arranged on so small a stage.

But February 13th, 1886, must be considered the culminating date of the modern dramatic movement. It was then that the New Theatre was opened—the theatre for which we had been waiting so long, and which was built mainly owing to the determination of two citizens of Oxford, Mr. Lucas and Mr. Drinkwater, to whom great assistance was given by Mr. W. L. Courtney, of New College, a warm supporter of the drama at Oxford. As if to em-

phasize the connection between the establishment of a good play-house with the
University dramatic renaissance, our Society was asked to open it with a performance of Shakspeare's " Twelfth Night,"
which was produced by Mr. Bourchier,
who played the *Clown* and recited a most
excellent and fantastic prologue in character,
contrasting the old and new state of the
drama at Oxford—the competition for pro-
logues was considerable 'on this occasion,
and a very good one by Mr. E. M. Wood
has since been printed; *Malvolio* was played
by Mr. E. H. Clark, *Sir Toby* by Mr. E. F.
Macpherson, *Sir Andrew* by Mr. Lechmere
Stuart, and the *Priest* by Mr. D. H. Maclean
(President of the Boat Club). The event
was greatly commented upon in the public
press—Mr. Burnand's article in *Punch* being
particularly happy—and a more enthusiastic
audience never assembled within the walls
of a theatre than on that night.

In the summer of 1886, in the Examination
Schools, before an audience which filled the

largest room in the building, and which included every shade and variety of academic thought and life, Mr. Irving delivered a lecture to Doctors, Proctors, and Under-graduates, on " English Actors." Nor did the paradox cease when the lecturer had closed his manuscript ; for thereupon the Vice-Chancellor (Mr. Jowett) made a speech in defence of the Drama, in which the translator of Plato's dialogues proved the falsity of his master's strictures on actors and acting.

In 1887 a new Vice-Chancellor (Dr. Bellamy, of St. John's) came in, and the O.U.D.S. gave an interesting performance in aid of a deserving Oxford charity—in which Lady Augusta Fane and the cele-brated amateur trio, Sir Spencer Ponsonby-Fane, Sir Henry de Bathe, and Mr. Quintin Twiss, gave great assistance—and in the Eights Week " Alcestis," in the original Greek, was performed, thus proving the strength and versatility of the Club ; and in the winter of the same year I made my

D

last appearance on the stage, previous to
being ordained, with my friend Mr. Arthur
Bourchier, in a duologue, written for us by
Mr. E. H. Whitmore, which we had played
for several years, bearing the appropriate
title of " Senior Wranglers."

————

Looking back on the past eight years, I
cannot help feeling thankful for what has
taken place in Oxford in respect of the
Drama.   The very opposition has had its
good effect, for it has prevented any hasty
decision on the subject.   The present recognition of the Drama has been arrived at
after careful thought, objections having been
well weighed on both sides.   The result is
that what has been achieved is likely to be
permanent.   It only remains for all Oxford
people, Graduates and Undergraduates, to
do their best to keep what they have got
good and blameless, and never to let any
cause of regret arise for what has been
done.

May I also add that the best way that Oxford actors can justify their existence is by unselfishly sharing their good things with those who are not so fortunately placed. Of late years, Oxford men of culture, Oxford musicians, Oxford cricketers, and Oxford oarsmen, have come down to East London and other poor neighbourhoods and have made a practical use of their talents for the benefit of others.   Let Oxford actors do the same !

J. G. ADDERLEY.

Printed by E. B. DOE, 126A, High Street, Oxford.

Printed in Great Britain
by Amazon

87543590R00031